SEEK TRUTH

GO WITHIN

SO SHALL YOU KNOW THYSELF

Emerald Shamira

MAGIC

of

LIFE

POEMS
by
EMERALD SHAMIRA

Copyright © 2017 Cheryl Weber (Author), Nicole Valega and Ryan Weber (Claimants).
All rights reserved. No portion of this book may be reproduced, distributed, or transmitted in any form or by any means, or stored in a database or retrieval system, without prior written permission of the publisher.

ISBN: 978-0-692-38525-8

THE BOOK COVER IS
INFUSED WITH LIQUID LOVE
IN SILENCE FEEL THE VIBRATIONS
OF FLAMES OF LOVE
FLOW THROUGH YOUR HEART
THIS ENERGY VORTEX WEAVES
THE MATRIX OF
ONE HUMAN FAMILY
HEART TO HEART

DEDICATION

This book of sacred poems is dedicated to my family. Thank you for your love and support.

To each of us who honor life's journey to remember we are one human family and recognize our hearts are united through the universal heart beating in synchronicity.

IN MEMORY

Our beloved mom left our lives all too soon. This creation was such a cherished passion for her these past years, bringing her so much joy. Unfortunately, she passed away before it got to publishing. In honor of her we want to be sure it is shared with those that love her, and anyone else whose life these poems are meant to touch. We love you mom, nana, sister, aunt & friend.

CONTENTS

INTRODUCTION
ELEMENTS
CONSCIOUSNESS OF LANGUAGE
SACRED GEOMETRY OF LANGUAGE

SPACE/SPIRIT

I AM ME BECAUSE OF YOU
HEART TO HEART
LIGHT & LOVE
BELOVED ONE
CHILDREN OF LIGHT
DANCE IN THE LIGHT
CODES OF THE UNIVERSE
SELF-LOVE
I AM A PORTAL
ESSENCE OF PEACE
SPARK OF LIFE
I AM GOLDEN LIGHT
INSTRUMENT OF PEACE
SACRED GEOMETRY
BREATH OF LIFE
STAR BEING
INVISIBLE BRIDGE
PASSAGES
DIVINE MATRIX
SUN LIGHTS OUR PATH
ILLUMINATION
POINTS OF LIGHT
SONG IN MY HEART
UNIVERSAL LAWS

FIRE

MY HEART'S LOVE
LOVE ELIXIR
LANGUAGE OF LOVE
SPIRAL OF LOVE
FLAME OF LIFE
MASTERS OF OUR UNIVERSE
MYSTIC MASTER
IGNITE YOUR FLAME
FLAME OF LOVE
ETERNAL LOVE
HOLOGRAM OF LANGUAGE
COUNCIL OF PEACE
PASSION
WHAT WILL YOU CHOOSE?
MASTERPIECE OF THE LIVING WORD
PATH OF LOVE
FREEDOM LIVES
I LOVE MYSELF
TAHRIR EGYPT
HAITI, YOU ARE GRACE
AWAKENING
NOW IS THE MOMENT
ISRAEL

EARTH

CEREMONIAL DANCE
LIVING UNIVERSE
EARTH RITUAL
NATURE'S MAGIC
STELLAR GATEWAY
I AM ONE WITH NATURE
LAND IS PEACE
CITIES OF LIGHT
GAIA
CYPRESS TREE
PARADOX OF LIFE
LAW OF CREATION
MESSAGE FROM EARTH
DANCE OF THE UNIVERSE
HAITI, WE LOVE YOU
STEWARDSHIP OF EARTH
TREE BY THE OCEAN
DAMASCUS
EARTH'S HEART
HEAVEN ON EARTH

AIR

SEEKER OF TRUTH
I AM THE UNIVERSE
ORACLE
HEART'S GIFT
LOVE IS JUSTICE
MYSTERY OF LIFE
INVISIBLE
BUTTERFLY
COOCON OF LIFE
SPIRIT OF PEACE
MAGIC OF LIFE
KNOW THYSELF

VEIL OF PERCEPTION
FREEDOM
NELSON MANDELA
DIVINE ORDER
SOAR LIKE AN EAGLE
PAINTING
INVISIBLE KNOWING
HUMMINGBIRD
ALCHEMY OF PEACE

WATER

COMMANDER OF OUR SHIP
SEA SHELL
SEA OF LOVE
LIFE IS A CHOICE
LIVE LIFE
SACRED ESSENCE
SECRETS OF LIFE
PHILANTHROPY
CONSCIOUSNESS OF UNITY
TRUTH
SACRED POLITICS
LIBERATION
JUSTICE
VEIL IS LIFTED
LEADERSHIP
MYSTICISM
MUSE
JUST BE
TRUE POWER
MIRRORS OF MY HEART
GRATITUDE
SACRED MISSION
PURPOSE OF LIFE

INTRODUCTION

The poems in the **MAGIC OF LIFE** are the vibrations of universal intelligence activating our cellular memory of who we are. When you read the poems, feel the energy flow through your body, and allow the vibration to harmonize you with the universal dance of life. Life flows through us, not to us. We are holograms of the universe. **WE ARE THE MAGIC OF LIFE.**

When the poems appear to me, I hear words, see pictures and feel the vibration of the words. They come in complete poems, sometimes three at a time. I do not think to write a poem, they flow through me.

I have always been drawn to ancient languages and the power of words. One of my gifts to the world is the wisdom of language. I understand the vibrational power of words and significance of what we speak. Know we are co-creating our reality with the energy of our thoughts, words, feelings and actions.

5 ELEMENTS OF NATURE & LIFE

The **MAGIC OF LIFE** is divided into the 5 elements of nature and life. Humanity is intrinsically woven through the 5 elements of nature and life, the truth is there is no separation. This is the mystery and magic of life. The 5 elements explain how the human body is in harmony with nature.

The platonic solids, basic shapes of sacred geometry, are five three-dimensional geometrical forms of which all faces are alike. Each platonic solid represents one of the five elements of creation: tetrahedron – fire, cube – earth, octahedron – air, dodecahedron – spirit/space and icosahedron – water. These geometric forms direct nature. All living cells hold the universal codes. Sacred geometry of language and yoga activate the codes.

ELEMENT OF SPIRIT/SPACE

Spirit is the inner space that holds everything together and provides the foundation for the 4 primary elements of fire, water, earth and air to interact. Spirit is the "spark of life", our connection to source. Space is the binding force of the universe between these elements. Space is the spectrum of vibration and sound that orchestrate the magic of nature and life. The magical power of spirit/space is the alchemy of LIGHT, illuminating life's path.

ELEMENT OF FIRE

Fire is form without substance, the invisible energy that purifies, cleanses and transforms. Fire is the flame of love, passion and strong desire. The magical power of fire is transmutation, the phoenix rising from the ashes.

ELEMENT OF EARTH

Earth is the foundation of which all seeds spring forth and is the mother of fertility. She is the realm of knowledge, wisdom and creation. The magical power of earth is manifestation into matter.

ELEMENT OF AIR

Air is the "breath of life." Fire needs air/wind to burn and purify. Air and fire are invisible and transforming. Air symbolizes mobility and dynamic universal power. The magical power of air is "to know", visualization, imagination, inspiration and freedom.

ELEMENT OF WATER

Water is the lifeblood for all living things. Water is the liquid space of matter, source of life and regeneration. Water is the energy of "go with the flow" and graces the earth with beauty. The magical power of water is "to dare" to dream.

Many poems fit under more than one element, so I included each poem within the element that appeared to me first.

CONSCIOUSNESS OF LANGUAGE

This book is written in conscious language coded with sacred geometry. Thus, you will be more conscious of how you navigate your personal life, community, work and outer world. You will have insights to assist with communication and writing you do. You will have a deeper understanding of how life flows through you, not to you. If you select a few poems as mantras, as a daily practice, you will have a new listening in all aspects of life, giving you a higher consciousness to create reality with. This wisdom reconnects you to your divine essence to remember WHO YOU ARE and see the invisible. When we transform ourselves from within, we transform the world. We truly are the CHANGE WE SEEK IN THE WORLD.

Being conscious of language and sound starts in the heart, radiating out impacting how humanity writes local, national and global documents with this wisdom transforming how humanity lives in the NOW MOMENT. We are the masters of our reality!

This magic of language activates us to remember we are one human family, not separate. Know the creation of reality lives in the present moment! Not in the past or future. The words we speak give physical form to reality. The words I AM bring us into the present moment. I AM declares you know who you are. Even if you do not believe it, if you say the words, the vibration in your cells resonates with your true essence. This is personal power activating your higher self. I AM is the portal connecting our heart/mind to the universal heart/mind. This is the MAGIC OF LIFE. When a person speaks I AM other people know if it is so by the energy vibrating forth. If it is so the energy connections heart to heart.

This is a brief summary of consciousness of language. For further information visit www.emeraldshamira.com.

SACRED GEOMETRY OF LANGUAGE

Sacred geometry is the "language" of creation and governs the structures of matter. These sacred patterns design everything in reality. The patterns are symbolic of the principle of oneness, the inseparable relationship of each piece of the whole, which exists at the foundation of all life. These repeating geometric patterns form pure energy into matter creating our physical bodies, plants and animals, and all life forms in the universe, such as the planets and stars. Music, architecture, art, alphabets and light are equations and harmonics of sacred geometry.

Sacred geometry is the portal to higher dimensions of consciousness, awakening the innate wisdom of our cells to connection with the universal mind/heart. As members of the human family we weave our unique genius of this matrix. Imagine a web of golden threads connecting all life. Sacred geometry is the grid matrix, the patterns linked through a web. As a grid collapses, everything in the hologram will end. Every cell in our body is a blueprint of the universe. Prisms of light create the holograms of experience to remember who we are. The paradox of life is that the whole/oneness of humanity is only visible when each of us looks through the lens of the hole and sees the LIGHT. This is where infinite possibilities live and become visible. This is where we remember WE ARE ONE. Herein we navigate the highway of life to redesign new realities.

The first time I saw "fire script" over letters, my body resonated with the vibrations and my heart knew they held divine wisdom. The "fire script" is the language of flame sacred geometries, the physics linking consciousness and the physical, weaving the fabric of life. "Fire script" is encoded with symbols that awaken consciousness. This is based on sacred geometries, which are sacred universal patterns of spirals used in the design of everything in our reality, which is continuously spinning reality. Words and names resonate at vibrational frequencies. Alphabets of language link our inner wisdom with our outer world of expression. Language is not just a tool for communication, the letter forms themselves are encoded with the knowledge of life and consciousness. Within language lives our reality. Life is a dance with the universe and words dance giving form to reality. The sounds of language vibrate in our cells and letters of sacred language penetrate the soul of the reader. When our senses are activated, we give life to our dreams. This is how we create physical form.

The ancient Egyptians and sages of India taught that yoga was a necessary practice for activating ourselves. In yoga the asanas move our bodies in and out of geometrical postures that realigns our physical forms with higher levels of consciousness. Sacred geometry of language activates our bodies and consciousness as through yoga. Thus, life flows through us, not to us.

SPACE

SPIRIT

I AM ME BECAUSE OF YOU

IT IS THE RESPONSIBILITY OF EACH OF US
   TO REMEMBER "WE ARE"
     INTRINSICALLY CONNECTED
THERE IS NO SEPARATION
   ONE HUMAN FAMILY
     WE EACH HAVE UNIQUE GIFTS
OUR UNIQUENESS IS THE STRENGTH
   OF EACH THREAD THAT WEAVES
     THE TAPESTRY OF HUMANITY

THIS IS THE PARADOX OF HUMANITY
   MANY VOICES, ONE SONG
   MANY COLORS, ONE RAINBOW
   DIVERSITY IS STRENGTH
     OF THE HUMAN SPIRIT
WHEN WE REMEMBER WE EXIST
   BECAUSE OF EACH OTHER
WE ARE THE MYSTERY OF LIFE
   IT IS SO...

HEART TO HEART

DANCE WITH ME
   ON THE OTHER SIDE OF THE VEIL
JOIN ME
   AND THE ENERGIES OF THE COSMOS
INVISIBLE FORCES OF NATURE
   AND EARTH HERSELF

YOU HOLD GREAT LIGHT
YOUR DREAMS
   ARE YOUR REALITY
YOUR BODY IS THE INSTRUMENT
   OF YOUR PHYSICAL MANIFESTATION

TRUST THE UNIVERSE
WE WEAVE OUR PART
   OF THE HUMAN MATRIX
OUR DIVINE ESSENCE
   TRANSMUTES HEART TO HEART

LIGHT & LOVE

WHITE GOLDEN LIGHT ACTIVATES
   YOUR HEART TO OPEN
TO REMEMBER INFINITE FREEDOM
   WHEN YOU WERE EXPANSIVE ENERGY
FREE TO EXPRESS IN SPIRALS
   OF BRILLIANT LIGHT
FEEL LOVE CARESS YOUR HEART
   RADIATING BEAMS OF LIGHT
FREE YOUR LOVE TO DANCE
   AND MERGE WITH UNIVERSAL LOVE
THE MOST POWERFUL FORCE
   IN THE UNIVERSE
THIS COSMIC DANCE WEAVES
   THE LIVING MATRIX OF YOUR NEW REALITY
YOU ARE A BEING OF LIGHT AND LOVE
   FINDING YOUR WAY HOME

BELOVED ONE

I INVITE YOU ON A MYSTICAL JOURNEY
  INTO THE DEPTH OF YOUR SOUL
TO EXPERIENCE YOUR DIVINITY
  AND UNITY WITH THE UNIVERSE
THE UNIVERSAL PRESENCE
  LIVES IN YOUR HEART
REMEMBER WHO YOU ARE
  THE BELOVED ONE

CHILDREN OF LIGHT

YOU ARE THE GUIDING LIGHT
  FOR HUMANITY
YOU ILLUMINATE THE PATH
  FOR US TO LIVE IN HARMONY
YOU SHOW THE WAY
  TO OUR HEARTS

YOU BRING GREAT WISDOM
  TEACHING HUMANITY
YOUR INNOCENCE IS YOUR GIFT
  REMINDING US WHO WE ARE
FOR YOU REMEMBER
  WHERE YOU CAME FROM

YOUR HEART TELLS THE TRUTH
  IF WE LISTEN
YOU DANCE
  WITH THE UNIVERSE
SPINNING THE ENERGY
  IN A SPIRAL OF LOVE

YOU COME IN MANY COLORS
   SPEAKING MANY LANGUAGES
YOU CREATE THE PERFECT RAINBOW
   COLORS BLENDING IN UNITY
WE HEAR THE HARMONY OF YOUR VOICES
   AS YOU LIGHT UP THE SKY

THROUGH YOUR EYES
   WE SEE THE MAGIC
YOU HEAR THE VOICES OF NATURE
   YOU ARE THE MAGIC OF LOVE
YOU SPEAK THE MYSTERIES OF LIFE
   A BREATH OF FRESH AIR

DANCE IN THE LIGHT

I SEE THE SPARKS DANCE IN THE LIGHT
MIND AND HEART ALIGN
I ACCESS MY HEART'S WISDOM
INTUITION FLOWS FORTH
I TAKE EMOTIONAL RESPONSIBILITY
COMMITTED TO HONOR ALL HUMANITY
MY HEART MERGES WITH MY SPIRIT
I LOVE MY AUTHENTIC SELF
MY ENERGY FIELD EXPANDS
CONNECTED TO UNIVERSAL CONSCIOUSNESS

ENERGY OF HUMANITY IS TRANSFORMING
LOVE AND COMPASSION RADIATE FORTH
I AM A PERSONAL TRANSISTOR
HOLDING THE SPACE
  FOR UNITY CONSCIOUSNESS
I FEEL INNER PEACE
EMBRACING OUR UNIQUE GIFTS
I REMEMBER...
  HUMANITY IS ONE WITH EARTH
  I AM ONE WITH THE GLOBAL HEART
  BEING LOVE AND UNITY

CODES OF THE UNIVERSE

CODES OF THE UNIVERSE
ACTIVATE OUR CELLS
SYNCHRONIZE US IN UNITY
REIGNITE MAGIC IN LIFE
RECONNECT US TO OUR INNER POWER

RIDE THE WAVES OF VIBRATIONAL ECHOS
HEAR THE VIBRATIONAL WHISPERS
FEEL THIS ENERGY FILL OUR CELLS
SEE THE INVISIBLE
SEE INFINITE POSSIBILITIES

THE DANCE OF THE UNIVERSE
FLOWING THROUGH US
IGNITING OUR PASSION
CALLING US FORTH
THE MAGIC IS IN EACH OF US

THIS MAGIC IS LOVE
THE INVISIBLE FORCE
RADIATING OUR LIGHT
INTO THE WORLD
REMINDING US THERE IS NO SEPARATION
ONE SOURCE LIGHTS OUR PATH

SELF-LOVE

SELF-LOVE IS THE PATH TO INNER PEACE
   HOLD YOURSELF IN THE GRACE OF LOVE
INNER PEACE LEADS TO DEEP TRUTHS
   TRANSCENDING TIME AND SPACE
SEE THROUGH CONCEPT AND THEORY
   SEE THE INVISIBLE
SIMPLICITY OF THE POWER OF LOVE
   IS THE PATH TO CLARITY

LIGHT OF LOVE IS SO BRILLIANT
   DEFUSING DARKNESS
HOLD OPPOSING VIEWS
   IN THIS SACRED SPACE
UNCONDITIONAL LOVE IN OUR HEARTS
   THE VIBRATION OF ONE HUMAN FAMILY
SELF-LOVE IS THE CHANGE
   WE SEEK IN THE WORLD

I AM A PORTAL

I AM THAT I AM
  I AM A CHILD OF THE UNIVERSE
I AM ONE WITH EARTH ASCENSION
  I AM AWAKENING MY SACRED GEOMETRY
I FEEL THE RHYTHM OF MY CELLS
   SYNCHRONIZE MY BODY
      WITH THE COSMOS
I AM A PORTAL OF CRYSTALLINE ENERGY
   BRIDGING DIMENSIONS

I AM A TEMPLE WITHIN MY HEART
   GOD DWELLS IN ME AS ME
WE ARE ONE IN OUR HEARTS
   WHEN I FORGIVE MYSELF
THERE IS NO ONE TO FORGIVE
   SELF-LOVE IS THE MAGIC OF LIFE
I AM LOVE, I AM LIFE
I AM FREEDOM, I AM PEACE

ESSENCE OF PEACE

PEACE IS THE MAGIC OF LOVE
   IN OUR HEARTS THERE ARE NO BORDERS
THE GREATEST MYSTERY OF THE UNIVERSE
   SO PROFOUND THIS EXPERIENCE
UNITING ALL HUMANITY
   ONE GLOBAL FAMILY
PEACE LIVES WITHIN OUR HEARTS FIRST
   THEN GLOBAL PEACE IS POSSIBLE
WE WRITE PEACE DOCUMENTS
   BIRTHED FROM OUR INNER PEACE

THE LAW OF LOVE IS AVAILABLE TO ALL
   WHO SEEK THE TRUTH
TRUTH DOES NOT TAKE SIDES
   THERE IS NO RIGHT OR WRONG
TRUTH IS THE PATH TO FREEDOM
   THE TRUTH IS WE ARE ONE
WE ALL WANT THE SAME THING
   TO LIVE IN HARMONY AND PEACE
HEREIN LIES THE MYSTERY OF LOVE
   INVOKING COMPASSION AND FORGIVENESS

WE ARE BORN DIVINE BEINGS
   REMINDING EACH OTHER WHO WE ARE
WHEN WE TRULY CONNECT WITH OUR EYES
   AND GAZE UPON THE OTHER'S SOUL
BE OPEN TO TRUTH
   ALLOW YOUR EYES TO SEE GREAT WISDOM
MAY YOUR HUG SEND THE VIBRATION OF LOVE
   THIS EMBACE IS THE ALCHEMY OF UNITY
FEEL THE ENERGY FLOW THROUGH YOUR BODY
   MERGING AS ONE

SPARK OF LIFE

OUT OF THE MIST RISES CRYSTAL CLARITY
LIFE FLOWS THROUGH US
AS WE EMBRACE THE MYSTERY
LIFE LIVES FROM WITHIN
BLOSSOMING A NEW BEING
AS THE SEASONS AND ELEMENTS
ORCHESTRATE THEIR MAGICAL POWERS
SPIRIT/SPACE IS
   THE UNIVERSAL BINDING FORCE

ELEMENTS OF NATURE
VIBRATIONAL ENERGY FORCES
HARMONIZE NATURE AND LIFE
FIRE CLEARS
   THE PATH AND IGNITES PASSION
WATER IS
   REBIRTH AND DARES YOU TO DREAM
AIR IS
   "TO KNOW WITHOUT KNOWING"
EARTH IS
   MANIFESTATION INTO MATTER
SPIRIT'/SPACE IS
   THE SPARK OF LIFE

I AM GOLDEN LIGHT

I AM BATHED IN GOLDEN LIGHT
GOLD SPECKS DART ACROSS THE SKY
PASSING THROUGH MY BODY
FILLING EACH CELL
I GLOW IN THE LIGHT
THE LIGHT INFUSES ME
WITH HIGHER CONSCIOUSNESS

I SEEK HIGHER KNOWLEDGE
I SEE TRUTH
I FEEL LOVE
I AM HOLY
I AM THAT I AM
I AM ALL THAT IS
I AM THE MYSTERY OF LIFE

I KNOW
I AM A SPECK OF LIGHT
IN THE GREAT UNIVERSE
I AM A GOLDEN STRING
WEAVING MY UNIQUE SIGNATURE
IN THE GOLDEN MATRIX OF LIFE
I AM THE GOLDEN LIGHT

INSTRUMENT OF PEACE

I AM AN INSTRUMENT OF PEACE
   GUIDED BY THE LIGHT
I FINE TUNE MY INSTRUMENT
   WITH PRECISION
HARMONIZING WITH THE GLOBAL CHOIR

AS I WALK THE STREETS OF EARTH
   MAY MY LIGHT SHINE IN THE DARK
MAY MY LIGHT BE SO BRIGHT
   IT BLINDS PHYSICAL VISION
SO HUMANITY SEES FROM THE HEART

HEART VISION IS GUIDED BY LOVE
   I FEEL LOVE RADIATING FORTH
LOVE IS THE UNIVERSAL LANGUAGE
   WE EACH HAVE A UNIQUE FREQUENCY
I AWAIT OUR SYNCHRONICITY

SACRED GEOMETRY

SACRED GEOMETRY
   THE LANGUAGE OF CREATION
      IS THE FOUNDATION OF LIFE
GEOMETRIC PATTERNS
   CARRY THE CODES OF CREATION
SOUND VIBRATES MATTER
   INTO PHYSICAL MANIFESTATION
THROUGH VIBRATIONAL SEQUENCES

ANCIENT LANGUAGES
   WERE WRITTEN AND SPOKEN
      IN THIS SACRED WISDOM
NUMBERS AND ALPHABETS
   CRAFT LIVING LANGUAGE
SO MAGICAL THE UNIVERSAL LAWS
   OF LIFE AND STRUCTURES
      IN OUR GALAXY

BREATH OF LIFE

OUR PASSION LIGHTS THE TORCH
OUR SPARK IGNITES INNER WISDOM
CALLING US TO LEAD FROM WITHIN
THIS IS TRUE POWER
THE MASTERS OF OUR REALITY

WORDS ARE THE BREATH OF LIFE
GIVING FORM TO NEW REALITIES
FORGING THROUGH DARKNESS INTO LIGHT
TRANSMUTING ILLUSIONS
BUILDING NEW BRIDGES

IN OUR HEARTS THE FLAME GLOWS
NO OUTER FORCE CAN DIM OUR FLAME
TRANSMUTING FEAR INTO LOVE
LIGHTING THE PATH TO PEACE
TRUTH IS WE ARE ONE

SPIRITUAL MATURITY TAKES COURAGE
CONNECT TO UNIVERSAL SOURCE
SURRENDER TO INNER KNOWING
TRUST VIBRATIONAL WHISPERS
BE IN GRATITUDE FOR ALL
PASS THROUGH THE INVISIBLE DOOR
TO A FIELD OF INFINITE POSSIBILITIES

STAR BEING

WE ARE STAR BEINGS SHINING SO BRIGHT
WHERE WE WALK IN PHYSICAL FORM
WE LIGHT THE WAY HOME
WE HOLD THE SPACE FOR HUMANITY
TO REMEMBER WHERE WE CAME FROM
NO ILLUSIONS LIVE IN THE LIGHT
LIGHT ILLUMINATES THE PATH
TO ONENESS
THIS IS WHERE PEACE AND JOY LIVE

OUR MISSION IS CLEAR
JUST BE IN THE ETERNAL MOMENT
SHINE THE LIGHT
DARKNESS FADES
WE REMEMBER OUR CONNECTION TO EARTH
EARTH RETURNS TO PEACE
OUR LOVE TRANSCENDS FEAR
SUCH IS THE ALCHEMY OF LOVE
HEAVEN ON EARTH

INVISIBLE BRIDGE

I AM
SUPREME LIGHT ETERNAL
LIGHT RADIATING TRUTH
THROUGH THE WORD
I AM
SUPREME LIGHT ETERNAL
RADIATING LIGHT SO BRIGHT
SEE LIFE IS THE MYSTERY
I AM
SPIRIT, FIRE, EARTH, AIR AND WATER
MYSTICAL CREATOR OF LIFE
BALANCING UNIVERSAL FLOW
I AM
THOUGHT, WORD, FEELING AND ACTION
FORMING REALITY
WITNESS TRANSFORMATION
I AM
INVISIBLE BRIDGE
THROUGH AND WITHIN DIMENSIONS
HUMANITY EXPANDING INTO ONENESS

PASSAGES

CYCLES OF LIFE LEAD US HOME
   TO OUR HIGHER SELF
AS WE OPEN EACH GATE
   A NEW PATH BECOMES VISIBLE
EACH MOUNTAINTOP
   LEADS TO A NEW VALLEY
MIRAGES APPEAR IN THE SAND
   ILLUSIONS OF THE MIND
FOLLOW YOUR HEART
   THE INVISIBLE ROAD

YOUR NAVIGATOR IS LOVE
   THE WAY THROUGH THE MOUNTAINS
THE PATH IS SPIRAL
   YOU CHOOSE THE JOURNEY
RAVINES MAY BE TREACHEROUS
   TRUST YOUR INNER WISDOM
INTUITION IS YOUR MAGIC WAND
   ILLUMINATING NEW PASSAGES
ON THE PATH TO THE LIGHT
   VIVIDLY IGNITING YOUR TRUE SELF

DIVINE MATRIX

I AM THE BELOVED I SEEK
   I AM THE MAGIC UNFOLDING
THE HOLOGRAM OF THE UNIVERSE
   EXPRESSING IN EVERY CELL
THE DIVINE MATRIX OF LIFE
   WEAVING THE TAPESTRY OF LOVE

OUR RAINBOW BIRTHS A JEWEL TO BEHOLD
   SHIMMERING IN THE LIGHT
THE CRYSTALS IN OUR BODIES FEEL HARMONY
   BATHED IN THE ALCHEMY OF LOVE
VIBRATING IN RESONANCE
   WITH THE UNIVERSAL CELL
   WE ARE HOME, UNITED AS ONE

SUN LIGHTS OUR PATH

AS THE SUN LIGHTS OUR PATH
  SO WE LIGHT THE EARTH
    WITH OUR PRESENCE
SO WE RADIATE LOVE
    FLOWING THROUGH HUMANITY
    WEAVING THE MATRIX

SO THE CIRCLE OF LOVE
    CARESSING EARTH
      SYMBOLIZES ONENESS
OUR FLAME OF LOVE
    MELTS SEPARATION
    ECHOING INCLUSION

ILLUMINATION

BREATHE THE LIGHT
   FEEL IT ENGULF YOU
CLOSE YOUR EYES
   SEE FROM WITHIN
YOU WILL SEE
   THE MYSTERIES OF LIFE
ILLUMINATING YOUR PATH
   ALL IS REVEALED TO YOU!

POINTS OF LIGHT

THE POINT OF "BEING" ON EARTH
   IS TO RECOGNIZE OUR ONENESS
WE ARE SACRED ASPECTS
   OF THE CIRCLE OF LIFE
POINTS HAVE NO BEGINNING
   AND NO END
THE MOST PRIMAL LIGHT
   OF CONSCIOUSNESS
NATURAL LAWS LIVE WITHIN US
   REMINDING US OF INCLUSION
WHEN OUR POINTS OF LIGHT GLOW
   DARKNESS CANNOT PENETRATE
   OUR SPIRITUAL OMNIPRESENCE

SONG IN MY HEART

I HAVE A SONG IN MY HEART
   IT BEATS TO UNIVERSAL HARMONICS
I AM A PART OF YOU
   YOU ARE A PART OF ME
WE ARE PARTS OF ONE HUMAN FAMILY

UNIVERSAL LAWS

UNIVERSAL LAWS
   HOLD US TO A HIGHER LEVEL
     OF ACCOUNTABILITY
OUR CELLS RECOGNIZE
   THE VIBRATIONAL TONES
IT IS OUR CHOICE
   TO ANSWER THE CLARION CALL
TO COMMIT TO UNIVERSAL RESPONSIBILITY

FIRE

MY HEART'S LOVE

OUR HEARTS ARE CONNECTED
　TO THE UNIVERSAL HEART
WE BREATHE AS ONE
　UNITED FOR ETERNITY
THIS IS THE MAGIC OF LOVE
　DANCING IN SPIRALS

I CALL YOUR NAME
　I AWAIT YOUR EMBRACE
I FEEL YOUR PRESENCE
　YOU FILL ME WITH LOVE
OUR HEARTS BEAT AS ONE
　OUR ENERGY ENTWINED

LOVE ELIXIR

DIVINE LOVE IS SO
WHEN I LOVE MYSELF
I REMEMBER, I AM LOVE
AS LOVE, I LOVE
THUS, I AM LOVED
I REFLECT LOVE
THROUGH MYSELF TO OTHERS
HEREIN, IS THE MAGIC OF LOVE
THE PATH TO INNER POWER
THUS, PEACE IN THE WORLD
AS THE FLOWER OF THE HEART OPENS
LOVE ELIXIR FILLS THE AIR

LANGUAGE OF LOVE

LOVE IS UNIVERSAL
  SPEAKING TO THE HEART
AS WE HEAL FROM WITHIN
  WE RADIATE LOVE
WEAVING THE TAPESTRY
  UNITING HUMANITY
THE EARTH FEELS OUR LOVE
  AND IS AT PEACE

WE ARE THE MASTERS OF OUR DESTINY
  WE CHOOSE OUR PATH OF LIFE
THIS IS NATURE'S SECRET
  SPEAKING TO OUR SOULS
THE VIBRATION OF LOVE
  FORGING THE WAY
THE ENERGY GUIDING FORCE
  TO PEACE WITH THE UNIVERSE

AS THE STARS ABOVE
  GAZE ON EARTH
THEY SEE THE HALO OF LOVE
  A FLAME OF GOLDEN GLOW
IGNITING THE WAY
  BACK HOME TO OUR DIVINITY
ENGULFING HUMANITY
  WITH ENDLESS POSSIBILITIES

SPIRAL OF LOVE

BODIES MERGING, PURE ENERGY FLOWING
   THE HOLOGRAM OF THE UNIVERSAL SOUL
ON THE BATTLEFIELDS OF THE WORLD
   HEALING HATRED, ANGER AND FEAR

TRAVELING THE WORLD
   HOLDING THE HANDS OF THE CHILDREN
SINGING IN THEIR OWN LANGUAGES
   SING THE SAME SONG
HUMANITY, AN EVOLUTIONARY SPIRAL OF LOVE
   A SPIRAL SPINNING WITHIN A PYRAMID
THIS PYRAMID A TRIUNE OF HUMAN EXPERIENCES
   BIRTHING HARMONY AND PEACE

FLAME OF LIFE

THE FLAME OF LIFE
BURNS DEEP IN THE EARTH
I AM THE KEEPER OF THE FLAME
I GUARD THE FLAME WITH MY PRESENCE

I AM THE ESSENCE OF THE SUN
MY RADIANCE ILLUMINATES THE WORD
THE WORD GIVES FORM TO ORDER
MY GOLDEN EYES SEE WISDOM IN THE LIGHT

MASTERS OF OUR UNIVERSE

WE EACH HAVE A PASSION
THAT IGNITES OUR GREATNESS
THE MYSTERIES OF THE UNIVERSE
 CALL FORTH OUR WISDOM

AS OUR SPARKS DANCE ACROSS THE SKY
WE UNITE AS ONE BRILLIANT LIGHT
A TORCH OF COURAGE
WE REMEMBER...
WE ARE THE MASTERS OF OUR UNIVERSE

MYSTIC MASTER

I AM A MYSTIC MASTER
  GRACED BY THE DIVINE
I AM A PORTAL OF LIGHT
  SPIRALING A NEW REALITY
I AM AN ETHERIC HOLOGRAM
  IN A CRYSTAL PYRAMID
I SHIFT PARADIGMS
  WITH POETIC MUSICAL ALCHEMY
I HOLD THE SACRED CODES
  ANCHORING THE NEW EARTH

I SEEK THE MYSTERIES OF LIFE
  I REMEMBER...
I AM A GOLDEN THREAD
  WEAVING LIFE'S TAPESTRY
I WALK IN MANY DIMENSIONS
  TO AN UNKNOWN DESTINATION
I SEE THE INVISIBLE FROM AFAR
  TRUTH ILLUMINATES MY TORCH
I AM A MESSENGER
  FORGING A NEW PATH

IGNITE YOUR FLAME

IGNITE YOUR FLAME
   OF LIFE'S PURPOSE
YOU ARE A FLAME
   OF PEACE
IGNITE YOUR LIGHT

ASK THE DIVINE
THE WISDOM IS WITHIN
   YOUR HEART
YOUR HEART FLAME
   IS YOUR LIFE PURPOSE

FLAME OF LOVE

LOOK THROUGH THE EYES OF FEAR
   WHEN YOU ACCEPT WHAT IS TRUTH
WHAT YOU SEE WILL MELT
   BY THE FLAME OF LOVE
THIS IS THE CATALYST
   FOR TRANSFORMATION

ETERNAL LOVE

ETERNAL LOVE
   OUR CONNECTION TO THE SACRED
THE VIBRATION OF LOVE
   CALLED US TO EARTH
TO BIRTH THE NEW HUMANITY
   EMBRACING OUR UNITY
OUR SPIRITS LIVE THROUGHOUT ETERNITY
   THIS IS OUR SACRED JOURNEY

WE REMEMBER THE ANCIENT WISDOM
   RETURNING TO PURE ENERGY
OUR CELLS CARRY THE SECRET CODES
   TO TRANSMUTATION
AWAKING THE CRYSTALS IN OUR BODIES
   ACTIVATING OUR SPIRIT WITHIN

BEFORE WE CAME INTO FORM
   WE WERE SPIRALS OF ENERGY
MERGING AS ONE
   VIBRATING IN UNISON
FLICKERING IN SPACE
   FORMLESS FREEDOM
WE LEFT OUR HOMES
   TO TAKE HUMAN FORM

HOLOGRAM OF LANGUAGE

POETRY IS MAGICAL THINKING
   IN HOLOGRAPHIC LANGUAGE
THE FLAME GEOMETRIES
   HOLD THE KNOWLEDGE OF LIFE
DANCING OVER THE LETTERS
   SPEAKING IN "The Light"
THE CONSCIOUSNESS OF THE WORDS
   OPEN THE EYES OF HUMANITY

SACRED LANGUAGE SHAPED IN "Fire Script"
   PENETRATES THE SOUL OF THE READER
THE SOUNDS OF LANGUAGE
   VIBRATE IN OUR CELLS
BRIDGING CULTURAL BARRIERS
   AND GLOBAL COMMUNICATION
EACH CULTURE HAS A CONTRIBUTION
   TO THE EVOLUTION OF HUMANITY

COUNCIL OF PEACE

I AM A CRYSTAL PYRAMID
   HOLDING THE SPACE FOR HUMANITY
I HEAR THE VOICES OF THE CULTURES
   THEY EACH HAVE A UNIQUE VIBRATION
THE ENERGY MOVES AROUND THE PYRAMID
   CALLING FORTH THEIR TURN TO SPEAK

THE PYRAMID, THE VORTEX,
   IS THE VEHICLE OF TRANSMUTION
THE CRYSTAL HOLDS THE CHIMES
   OF THE GLOBAL CHOIR
IN UNISON THEY SOUND
   THE GIFTS THEY BRING TO THE CIRCLE

THIS IS THE COUNCIL OF PEACE
   GATHERED TO IGNITE THE FLAME
TO BIRTH THE GOVERNMENT OF LIGHT
   THE MASTER TEACHERS OF EARTH
IN COUNCIL THEY UNITE
   CALLED FORTH BY THE ANCIENT ONES

PASSION

PASSION IS MY GUIDING FORCE
   THE FIRE BURNING DEEP WITHIN
MY INNER WISDOM IGNITES THE FLAMES
   OF MY UNIQUE GIFT
MY CELLS ARE FILLED WITH EXCITEMENT

I DANCE IN THE GLOW OF THE SACRED FIRE
   I FEEL THE SYNERGY FLOW
THE UNIVERSE CALLS ME FORTH
   MY INNER VOICE SPEAKS TRUTH
MY PASSION IS MY SIGNATURE

WHAT WILL YOU CHOOSE?

WE HAVE MANY CHOICES
WHAT WILL YOU CHOOSE?
WILL YOU CROSS THE INVISIBLE LINE
COURAGE AND BOLDNESS GUIDE YOU
LET YOUR HEART LEAD
PASSION IS YOUR HIGHER SELF
IF YOU LISTEN
PASSION ALWAYS SPEAKS TRUTH
FEEL THE VIBRATION
WHEN WE ARE IN ALIGNMENT
OTHERS RESONATE

MASTERPIECE OF THE LIVING WORD

I AM THE TORCH THAT ILLUMINATES TRUTH
   BOLDNESS AND COURAGE ARE MY GUIDES
FIRE CODES OF WORDS IGNITE A NEW REALITY
   ETCHED ON PARCHMENT

THE GOLDEN SEAL IS MY MAGIC
   THE KISS OF THE DIVINE
THE THREADS OF GOLDEN LIGHT
   WEAVING THE FABRIC OF LIFE

THE SHARED LANDSCAPE OF HUMANITY
   IS THE CANVAS OF LIFE
UPON WHICH THE SOCIAL ARCHITECT
   CRAFTS THE MASTERPIECE OF THE LIVING WORD

PATH OF LOVE

OUT OF CHAOS COMES ORDER
   OUT OF DARKNESS COMES LIGHT
THE MYSTERIES OF LOVE,
   FORGIVENESS AND COMPASSION
GUIDE OUR WAY
   THROUGH THE DARKNESS TO LIGHT

LOVE ILLUMINATES TRUTH
   TRUTH SETS US FREE
OUR SACRED ACTIONS BIRTH A NEW WORLD
THE FIRE CODES OF OUR WORDS
   FORM A NEW REALITY

HUMANITY AND THE EARTH NOW
   LIVE IN HARMONY, PEACE AND PROSPERITY
WE HONOR OUR PLACE IN THE UNIVERSE

FREEDOM LIVES

FREEDOM LIVES
　IN BEING RESPONSIBLE TO EACH OTHER
FREEDOM OF SPEECH LIVES
　IN RESPECTING OPPOSING VIEWS
LISTENING IN SILENCE WITH OPEN HEARTS
KNOWING WE ALL WANT THE SAME THING

PEACE FIRST LIVES IN OUR HEARTS
　RADIATING LOVE INTO THE WORLD
THE VIBRATION OF LOVE
　THE MOST POWERFUL FORCE IN THE UNIVERSE
　MYSTICAL MAGIC IGNITING OUR HEART FLAMES
　UNITING HUMANITY HEART TO HEART

HUMANITY TAKES A QUANTUM LEAP
WHEN PEOPLE MASTER THE FORCE OF LOVE
　FEAR AND SEPARATION MELT
WHEN WE, THE PEOPLE, REMEMBER WE ARE ONE
WORLD PEACE IS SO…

I LOVE MYSELF

I LIVE FROM WHO I AM
I AM IN HARMONY WITH MY DIVINE ESSENCE
MY EYES ARE THE WINDOW TO MY SOUL
MAY MY EYES RADIATE LOVE

I LIVE FROM MY AUTHENTIC SELF
I SEE MYSELF THROUGH YOUR HEART
WHAT I SEE IN YOU IS WHAT I SEE IN MYSELF
OUR HEARTS BEAT AS ONE

MAY YOU FEEL MY LOVE
MERGE WITH YOUR HEART
I AM YOU, I LOVE YOU
I LOVE MYSELF

TAHRIR EGYPT

'TAHRIR" IS LIBERTY
   YOUR SACRED MISSION
YOUR FLAME IS IGNITED
   CAIRO IS BURNING
AS THE SPARKS FLY
   ACROSS THE MIDDLE EAST
YOU ARE THE CATALYST
   FOR THE CRADLE OF CIVILIZATION
YOU ARE THE HEART AND SOUL
   OF THE ARAB WORLD
EMBRACE TRANSFORMATION
   A NEW ERA OF LIFE AND LIBERTY
YOUR STAR SHINES BRIGHT
   BIRTHING A NEW REALITY

ANCIENT WISDOM
   BURNS IN YOUR HEARTS
YOU HAVE TRANSCENDED FEAR
   NOW EMBRACE LOVE
HEAL YOUR ANGER
   FEEL LOVE, BE LOVE
THIS IS YOUR TRUE POWER
   LET LOVE GUIDE YOUR ACTIONS
FREEDOM AND DIGNITY
   FIRST LIVES IN YOUR HEARTS
THIS IS YOUR GOLDEN OPPORTUNITY
   GOLDEN RAYS OF THE SUN EMBRACE
EGYPT THE SYMBOL OF LIBERTY
   YOU WERE BIRTHED FOR THIS DAY

THE PHARAOH HAS FALLEN
   FREE EGYPT LIVES
      LEADING ARAB LIBERTY
YOUR CHANTS OF UNITY
   AND DANCE OF JUBILATION
      IS THE PATH FORWARD
YOUR CULTURAL LINEAGE
   HAS GUIDED YOU TO THIS MOMENT
      ALLOW ORGANIC EVOLUTION
YOUR CRY FOR FREEDOM
   VIBRATES ACROSS THE GLOBE
      WE HEAR YOUR VOICE
TAHRIR SQUARE IS YOUR PLATFORM
   YOUR HUMAN CHAIN FOR LIBERTY
      IS THE SYMBOL OF ONE HUMANITY
YOUR DREAMS ARE OUR DREAMS
   WE LOVE AND HONOR YOU
      WALK FREELY, BIRTH A NEW NATION

HAITI, YOU ARE GRACE

NO NAMES RECORDED
   YOUR ESSENCES LIVE IN OUR HEARTS
WE LOVE YOU THROUGHOUT ETERNITY
   NO NAMES RECORDED
WE FEEL THE TEARS IN YOUR EYES
WE STAND BY YOU
   YOU ARE NOT ALONE
WE WALK HAND AND HAND
   UNITED AS ONE

WE LIFT YOU UP
   MAY YOU RISE ABOVE
AS WE REBUILD HAITI
   WE REBUILD THE WORLD
YOUR SMILES LIGHT OUR HEARTS
   YOUR TENACITY GIVES US HOPE
LIFE IS A MYSTERY
   HAITI, YOU ARE THE SOUL

WE SEE YOUR HALO
   YOU ARE HUMANITY'S SAVING GRACE
YOUR HALO LIGHTS
   THE PATH FORWARD
WE FEEL YOUR EMBRACE
   YOU WON'T FADE AWAY
WE'RE AWAKNENED NOW
   WE LOOK INTO OUR HEARTS

AWAKENING

PURIFICATION FROM ILLUSION
  AWARENESS OF SELF
MERGING THE CYCLES OF TIME
  SPIRALING THROUGH THE VORTEX
RETURNING TO ONENESS
  A UNIVERSAL CITIZEN

NOW IS THE MOMENT

IN THE NOW MOMENT
IS THE MAGIC OF LIFE
THIS IS WHERE PEACE LIVES
WHEN OUR HEART VIBRATES PEACE
WE LINK WITH THE UNIVERSAL HEART
IN THIS MOMENT
WE TRANSCEND TIME AND SPACE

PEACE LIVES IN THE MOMENT
NOT SOME TIME IN THE FUTURE
BECOMING IS IN THE TIMELESS NOW
THE UNIVERSAL HOLOGRAM
HOLDS ALL POSSIBILITIES
WHERE COLLECTIVE CONSCIOUSNESS
IS "BEING PEACE IN THE MOMENT"

ISRAEL

HOLD YOUR HEARTS OPEN
REMEMBER...
   HUMANITY HAS ONE HEARTBEAT
ALL NATIONS
   PART OF THE GLOBAL COMMUNITY
TRUE ISRAEL IS NOT PHYSICAL,
   HISTORICAL, OR ETHNIC
IT IS THE ISRAEL
   OF ALL VIBRATING LEVELS OF LIGHT
EXPRESSING DIFFERENT LIGHT EMINATIONS
   OF HUMANITY
LIVING YHWH IS INFINITE
   NOT EXCLUSIVE
A DIMENSION OF TIME
   BEYOND HISTORICAL LINEAR TIME

WALLS OF SEPARATION DO NOT PROTECT
PEACE HAS NO BORDERS
YHWH GAVE LOVE TO TRANSMUTE FEAR
WHEN OUR HEARTS LOVE PEACE EMERGES
THIS IS THE OPPORTUNITY
   TO LIVE YHWH'S WORDS
BE A MODEL FOR THE WORLD
TRANSCEND THE WALLS OF FEAR
HEAL YOUR HISTORY
THEN YOU CAN HONOR YOUR DESTINY
TO EVOLVE
   HIGHER LEVELS OF CONSCIOUSNESS
MAY THE POWER OF LOVE
   IGNITE YOUR ACTIONS
LIVE IN GRACE AND LOVE

WHAT WILL ISRAEL CHOOSE?
PHYSICAL JERUSALEM
   OR SPIRITUAL JERUSALEM
NOT A PIECE OF LAND ON EARTH
   RATHER A HIGHER VIBRATION
AS HUMANITY EVOLVES
   TO A GREATER UNDERSTANDING OF THE LIGHT
   A HIGHER LOVE IS REVEALED
TEACHING NEW LAWS
   DEEPER WISDOM AND NEW GOVERNMENT
MAY ISRAEL ECHO JUBILATION
   A CELEBRATION OF ONENESS
THE HUMAN FAMILY CAN SIT
   AT THE TABLE OF PEACE

ONCE WRITTEN IN STONE
NOW THE DESERT SAND BLOWS
   PURIFYING THE EARTH
AS THE WINDS OF CHANGE
   SWEEP THE MIDDLE EAST
A FLAME IS IGNITED
   NEW POSSIBILITIES BORN
LET'S WRITE A NEW BEGINNING
   AN ERA OF GLOBAL PEACE

MAY THE LAND OF ISRAEL
BE THE LAND OF GLOBAL COMMUNITY
THE TRUE ISRAEL
   SCATTERED ACROSS THE EARTH
NOW TIME TO UNIFY THE HUMAN FAMILY
ONE UNIVERSAL HEART WITH MANY FACES
ONE HEART VIBRATING LOVE AND PEACE

EARTH

CEREMONIAL DANCE

I HEAR THE EARTH'S HEARTBEAT
   INSIDE OF ME
I LISTEN TO THE TONE
   AND FEEL THE VIBRATION
WATER OF THE RIVERS FLOW
   AS OUR BLOOD FLOWS
AS THE GRAPEVINES WEAVE
   UNDER THE EARTH
     AND REACH FOR THE SUN
THE SPIRAL OF LIFE
   CONNECTS US BELOW THE EARTH
     AND SPINS US ABOVE
THIS IS THE COSMOS DANCE
   CONNECTING US TO OUR GALACTIC FAMILY
THIS DANCE BRINGS US INTO BALANCE
   IN COSMIC BRILLIANCE

LIVING UNIVERSE

WE LEARN BY WATCHING NATURE
   OUR GREAT TEACHER
ACTING IN UNISON
   WE HONOR OUR LIFE PURPOSE
CONSCIOUS EVOLUTION
   BECOMING ONE UNIVERSAL BODY
BOTH MATTER AND ENERGY
   AT THE SAME TIME
THIS ORGANIC MYSTICAL EXPERIENCE
   IS PRIMORDIAL UNDERSTANDING
SCIENCE AND SPIRIT MERGING
   FORMING PERFECT UNION

INTELLIGENCE SELF-DESIGNING
   A NEW WORLD EMERGING
ALLOW YOUR DREAMTIME
   TO TAKE YOU ON A JOURNEY
IN THIS TRANSITION
   TO THE UNIVERSAL HUMAN
IN THE REALM OF SPIRIT
   VISION THE NEW CULTURE
OUR BODY IN COMMUNION
   FEELING THE COSMIC STREAM OF LOVE
THIS IS THE EARTH DANCE
   IN THE LIVING UNIVERSE

EARTH RITUAL

I GIVE GRATITUDE FOR ABUNDANCE
   AND NATURE'S MAGIC
FOR RESOURCES AND THE BIOSHERE
   HOLDING THE BALANCE OF LIFE
FOR PLANTS, ALL LIVING FOOD
   AND THE HERBS THAT HEAL
FOR THE WATER THAT SUSTAINS LIFE
   AND THE AIR WE BREATHE
I BOW TO YOUR MAGESTY
   AND THE CYCLES OF LIFE
I AM HUMBLED BY YOUR PRESENCE
   YOU ARE THE BREATH OF LIFE
YOU SUPPLY ALL OUR NEEDS
   WHEN WE HONOR YOUR GIFTS

NATURE'S MAGIC

NATURE'S POWER IS MAGICAL
   RIVERS ARE THE LUNGS OF THE PLANET
HER ECO-SYSTEM IS THE LIFE BLOOD
   FOR HUMANITY
HER BEAUTY AND MAJESTY
   GRACE THE EARTH

EARTH'S MOUNTAINS CAPPED IN WHITE SNOW
   SEND WATER TO THE OCEANS
OCEANS ARE THE ENVIRONMENT
   FOR THE ENERGY OF LIFE
NATURE'S POWER OF WIND AND RAIN
   PURIFY THE LAND, BIRTHING NEW LIFE

EARTH'S CYCLES ARE A SYMBOL
   OF FREEDOM AND CREATIVITY
HER PRIMORAL DANCE MOVES IN HARMONY
   HER MAGICAL WORLD UNFOLDING
EARTH'S MYSTERIES
   ARE THE SECRETS OF THE AGES

STELLAR GATEWAY

WHEN I HEAL SELF-PITY
I HEAL OTHERS
I VALUE MY SELF-WORTH
I FORGIVE MYSELF
I AM COMPASSION
I LIVE IN GRACE

I AM LIBERATED
TO CLIMB THE STELLAR GATEWAY
I ACCESS SACRED WISDOM
I LIVE MY HIGHER PURPOSE
I CHOOSE TO LIVE IN THE LIGHT
I CHOOSE TO HONOR MY GIFTS

I AM ONE WITH NATURE

AS I GAZE AT THE MOUNTAIN SILHOUETTE
    THE SUN SHINES its GOLDEN RAYS ON EARTH
THE CLOUDS FLOAT ACROSS THE SKY
    AT TIMES HIDING THE SUN
AS I STAND NEXT TO THE ANCIENT TREES
    I AM REMINDED OF LIFE'S MYSTERIES

I AM ONE WITH NATURE
    ONE SOURCE, MANY FORMS
I CREATE THE LANDSCAPE OF MY LIFE
    WITH MY UNIQUE SIGNATURE
AS THE UNIVERSE DESIGNS WITH PHI
    THE MOLECULAR STRUCTURES OF LIFE

LAND IS PEACE

PETRA, THE CITY OF STONE
   STANDS SO TALL
THE SACRED CITY OF THE SILK ROUTE
THOSE WHO TRADED IN PEACE
   ENTERED THE NARROW SIQ
THE STONE WAS CARVED
   SO WATER FLOWED DOWN THE SIQ
THOSE WHO DARE TO WALK HER ANCIENT STEPS
   LEAP AND FLY AS THOUGH THEY HAVE WINGS

THE CITY OF PEACE
   ON THE JORDAN RIVER
      HER LAND IS PEACE
FEEL THE VIBRATION OF PEACE
   RUN THROUGH YOUR BODY
KNOW THAT PROFOUND MAGIC
   IS POSSIBLE WHEN WE CONNECT
      WITH THE "LIFE-BLOOD"
         OF EARTH AND HUMANITY
THIS LAND, A BEACON IN THE MIDDLE EAST

CITIES OF LIGHT

SPIRALS OF ENERGY
  FLOW THROUGH THE EARTH
CONNECTING UP TO THE SKY
  CREATING VORTEXES OF ENERGY
PROTECTING THE CITIES OF LIGHT

THE CITIES OF LIGHT
  ARE ENERGY GRIDS
CREATED BY GLOBAL CITIZENS
  RADIATING LOVE AND PEACE
IN THESE GLOBAL COMMUNITIES
  HUMANITY BIRTHS A NEW WORLD
EARTH NOW TAKES ITS PLACE IN THE UNIVERSE

GAIA

THERE IS AN INTRINSIC CONNECTION
   BETWEEN HUMANITY AND EARTH
WE BREATHE THE SAME AIR
   DRINK THE SAME WATER

GAIA, MOTHER EARTH
   PROTECTS THE BALANCE OF LIFE
PROVIDES THE ENVIRONMENT
   THAT NUTURES OUR BODIES

AS THE HUMAN FAMILY
   WE ARE THE STEWARDS OF HER LAND
WHEN WE HEAL OUR BODY, MIND AND HEART
   WE HONOR THE EARTH

WHEN WE SPEAK WITH HER
   SHE HEARS OUR VOICE AND ANSWERS
WHEN WE ARE IN GRATITUDE
   SHE PROVIDES ABUNDANCE
THE RAINS REPLINISH EARTH'S LIFE

CYPRESS TREE

I AM A MOSAIC
   A MARVEL OF MAGNIFICENT BEAUTY
MY PRISTINE FORM
   BREATHTAKING TO BEHOLD
MY BRANCHES ARE ETCHED BY THE WIND
   THE FIERCE FORCE BECKONs THE OCEAN
MAKING ITS PRESENCE KNOWN
   TO THE LANDSCAPE
MY ROOTS ARE FIRM UNDERGROUND
   ENTWINING TO ANCHOR

SUCH A MASTERPIECE
   A SYMBOL FOR HUMANITY
HOW NATURE SUPPORTS US
   AS WE MERGE WITH THE TREE ROOTS
GROUNDING OURSELVES SOLID
   WITH ARMS STRETCHED TO THE SKY
RESILIENCE UNBENDING
   AS THE CYPRESS TREE

PARADOX OF LIFE

WHEN WE WALK
  IN GRACE AND LOVE
OUR HEARTS LEAD US
  TO THE PROMISE LAND
THIS IS NOT A PIECE OF LAND
  THE LAND IS AT PEACE

WHEN PEACE LIVES
  IN OUR HEARTS
THEN WE ARE AT PEACE
  WITH THE LAND
THE PROMISE LAND
  IS WITHIN OUR HEARTS

WHAT WE SEEK OUTSIDE
  LIVES INSIDE
THE ONLY PLACE TO GO
  IS WITHIN
THIS IS THE PARADOX OF LIFE
  THE HOLOGRAM OF REALITY

LAW OF CREATION

WE ARE OUR FEELINGS
SO WHEN YOU FEEL ANGRY OR SAD
SAY THANK YOU FOR THE FEELINGS
IMAGINE THEM IN A BUBBLE OF LOVE
AT THE SAME TIME
CONSCIOUSLY THINK THOUGHTS
OF WHAT YOU DESIRE IS SO
THIS IS THE LAW OF CREATION
YOU DO NOT NEED TO BELIEVE IT IS SO
FEELING "IT IS SO" IS THE CREATOR
THANK THE UNIVERSE FOR YOUR DESIRE
GRATITUDE IS THE VIBRATIONAL ENERGY
THAT CRYSTALLIZES REALITY
REMEMBER ... YOU ARE THE CREATOR
WE COCREATE THROUGH OUR FEELINGS

MESSAGE FROM EARTH

WHERE IS YOUR HUMANITY?
HAVE YOU LEARNED
   FROM NATURE AND THE INDIGENOUS ELDERS?
WHEN I SPEAK SOFTLY, DO YOU HEAR ME?
WILL YOU LISTEN
   NOW AS I RISE UP AND SOUND LOUDLY?
WILL YOU HEAR
   THE ECHOS OF THE COAL MINES
     AND OIL CRISES?
YOU BLAME ME
   FOR THE EARTHQUAKES AND HURRICANES
TRUTH IS
   YOUR DISCONNECT WITH SOURCE
     CALLS ME FORTH
IT IS HUMANITY'S
   LACK OF REVERENCE FOR THE EARTH
THAT INVOKES
   THESE FORCES AND I CRY OUT TO HUMANITY

THE EBB AND FLOW OF LIFE
   HOLDS THE SECRETS OF THE HEART
     NOT THE EGOCENTRIC MIND
THE ARROGANT
   WANT A QUICK FIX AND BLAME OTHERS
TRUTH IS
   YOU DO NOT LIVE IN HARMONY AND HUMILITY
DO NOT ASSUME YOU KNOW MY NATURE
   WHEN YOU DO NOT HOLD ALL LIFE SACRED
YOU DO NOT RESPECT
   THE WISDOM OF THE ECO-SYSTEM
     THAT SUSTAINS LIFE
     ON YOUR MAGNIFICENT HOME PLANET

WHEN YOU FIGHT WARS
   AND SHED BLOOD ON THE LAND
   DESECRATE EARTH'S RESOURCES
   CREATE SEPARATION WITH POVERTY/SLAVERY
   MAKE DEPENDENCY ON OIL A SECURITY ISSUE
HUMANITY IS REFLECTING
   ON THE OUTSIDE WHAT LIVES INSIDE
THUS I CRY OUT, "COME HOME TO YOUR HEART"
AND RECONNECT
   WITH OUR UNIVERSAL INTELLIGENCE
HUMANITY IS THE BRIDGE TO RESTORE BALANCE
LIVE IN HARMONY
   "LIVING IN LOVE RADIATING FROM OUR HEARTS"

IN THE VASTNESS OF THE UNIVERSE
   LIFE IS TO BE HONORED SACRED
THIS INCLUDES WATER, LAND AND AIR
   INTRINSICALY CONNECTED TO SUSTAIN ALL LIFE
HUMANITY IS A PART OF THIS BIOSPHERE
   NOT THE DOMINATE FORCE
   WEAVING THE WEB OF LIFE IN THE UNIVERSE
THE MYSTIC OF NATURE LIVES IN THE HEART
   AND SPEAKS THE SAME LANGUAGE
      TO HUMAN, TREE, BREATH OF AIR
      AND DROP OF WATER
LISTEN TO THE UNIVERSAL HEARTBEAT
   AND FEEL THE RHYTHM

DANCE OF THE UNIVERSE

I AM THE DANCE OF THE UNIVERSE
   WEAVING THE FABRIC OF LIFE
THE SACRED GEOMETRIES OF LIFE DANCE
   SPINNING THE ESSENCE OF LIFE

WE EMBODY DIFFERENT FORMS
   OUR SOURCE IS THE SAME
EACH WITH UNIQUE GIFTS
   OUR DANCE IS VERTICAL
IN OUR HEARTS WE ARE ONE
   LIVING IN HARMONY

HAITI, WE LOVE YOU

WE HONOR YOUR SACRIFICE
   TO OPEN THE HEART OF HUMANITY
YOU HAVE CALLED FORTH
   COMPASSION, SHARING AND UNITY

AS THE EARTH SPEAKS TO US
   YOU HAVE CALLED FORTH LOVE
THE GLOBAL COMMUNITY IS UNITING
   IN PASSION, COMMITMENT AND VISION

STREWARDSHIP OF EARTH

EAT OF THE EARTH
   NURTURED BY THE SUN
HEAL YOUR BODY
   WISDOM FLOWS THROUGH YOU
REMEMBER WHO YOU ARE
   ONE WITH THE EARTH
IN UNISON WE BIRTH PEACE
   WE ARE THE STEWARDS OF THE EARTH

TREE BY THE OCEAN

I AM A PILLAR OF STRENGTH
   TOWERING SO TALL
MY ROOTS WEAVE TO HOLD ME UP
   AS THE WINDS RAGE
MY BRANCHES SWAY IN THE BREEZE
   CALLING TO NATURE
SINGING IN HARMONY
   UNBENDING IN UNISON

DAMASCUS

ROAD TO DAMASCUS
   LIGHT SHINING WITH TRUTHS
SYMBOLIZING HUMANITY'S
   GLOBAL CIVIL WAR
NATIONAL CIVIL WARS ARE REFLECTIONS
   OF THE ILLUSION OF SEPARATION

ROAD TO DAMASCUS
   LABYRINTH OF LIFE
SYMBOLIZING TRANSFORMATION
   TURNING POINT IN ONE'S LIFE
MAY THE UNIVERSAL HEART
   BE OUR GUIDE THROUGH THE MAZE

YOU ARE THE THIRD SYMBOLIC MESSAGE
   TO HUMANITY
YOUR SACRED LAND
   OF HIGHER CONSCIOUSNESS
     HAS GIVING THE CLARION CALL
WILL HUMANITY CHOOSE
   TO STAND IN THE LIGHT
     UNITED AS ONE

EARTH'S HEART

THE SOURCE OF MY SPIRIT
  IS DRAWN FROM THE EARTH'S HEART
I AM ONE WITH THE EARTH
  THE EARTH'S HEART IS BALANCE

WHEN I LEARN MY BALANCE
  I AM IN BALANCE WITH THE EARTH
THIS IS THE SECRET OF THE LAW OF HARMONY
  MAY HUMANITY REMEMBER....
    OUR ONENESS IN HEART

HEAVEN ON EARTH

MYSTICAL LAWS GOVERN OUR LIVES
  THEY BECKON US FORWARD
SACREDNESS IN OUR HEARTS
  AND WISDOM GUIDES US
CALLING US HOME
  TO CREATE HEAVEN ON EARTH

AIR

SEEKER OF TRUTH

I AM A MYSTIC MASTER
 I CAME DOWN FROM THE MONASTARY
TO LIVE AND WALK IN THE WORLD
 TO EXPERIENCE HUMANITY

I AM A SOCIAL ARCHITECT
 DRAFTING A BLUEPRINT
A NEW MAP FOR HUMANITY
 TO WALK A NEW PATH

I AM A SEEKER OF TRUTH
 THE TRUTH SETS US FREE
TRUTH COMES FROM WITHIN
 FREEDOM IS A STATE OF BEING

I AM THE UNIVERSE

DANCE WITH ME
   CLOSE YOUR EYES
   FEEL MY PRESENCE
I SURROUND YOU
   AND I AM YOU

I AM THE WIND AND RAIN
   THE AIR YOU BREATHE
   THE WATER YOU DRINK
THE FOOD NURTURING YOUR BODY
   THE EARTH YOU WALK UPON

YOU ARE THE CREATOR
   AND THE MIRACLE
THIS IS MAGICAL POWER
   THE SECRET OF ANCIENT WISDOM
YOUR OUTER WORLD
   IS A REFLECTION OF YOUR INNER WORLD

AS WE TRAVERSE THE JOURNEY CALLED LIFE
   YOU AND I ARE ONE
THE MAGIC OF LIFE IS LOVE
FOR IN LOVE
   THE ESSENCE OF ONENESS IS SO
ONE TRUTH, ONE REALITY!

ORACLE

I AM AN ORACLE
I AM ANGEL AND WARRIOR
I AM INFINITY AND INNOCENCE
I AM AN ENIGMA
   A HOLOGRAPHIC GODDESS
I DANCE IN YOUR HEART
   IGNITING YOUR PASSION
I AM A REFLECTION OF YOU
   SEE MY MAJESTY

MY WINGS SPAN THE UNIVERSE
   LIFTING THE VEILS OF ILLUSION
FEEL MY PRESENCE IN THE WIND
   MY SOUL TOUCHS THE SKY
HEAR MY SILENT ECHO IN YOUR EARS
   WE ARE UNITED IN ETERNAL LOVE
HEAR MY CHANT
   WORDS OF THE UNIVERSAL HEART
MY GAZE PIERCES
   THE WINDOW OF YOUR SOUL
SEE MY EYES SPEAK TO YOU
   THE MYSTERIES OF LIFE

BEHOLD MY MAGIC
   AS I AWAKEN YOUR SOUL
I AM A DREAM
   A VISION FROM ON HIGH
I AM THAT I AM
   A SPARK OF THE DIVINE
AS I DART ACROSS THE SKY
   I LIFT YOU UP
I BOW TO YOU
   I BEHOLD YOUR MAJESTY

HEART'S GIFT

LOVE AWAKENS MY HEART
ACTIVATING MY MIND
TRANSMUTING ILLUSIONARY THOUGHTS
RELEASING BELIEFS
EXPANDING HORIZONS
UNLIMITED POSSIBILITIES BECOME VISIBLE

MY HEARTBEAT HAS A NEW TUNE
I AM IN RESONANCE
  WITH THE UNIVERSAL HEART
I AM GRATEFUL FOR MY HEART'S GIFT
  OF ETERNAL LIFE
FREEDOM LIVES IN MY HEART
NOW I AM FREE IN THE WORLD
NOW I CREATE A NEW LIFE

LOVE IS JUSTICE

TO KNOW LOVE
IS TO BE LOVE
WHEN WE LOVE ALL OUR PARTS
WE BECOME WHOLE
THE PARTS ARE DUALITY
UNITY LIVES WITHIN DUALITY
ONCE WHOLE, LOVE EMERGES
AS LIGHT ONLY GLOWS IN DARKNESS
DUALITY IS THE VESSELL FOR LOVE
SURRENDER TO DUALITY

LOVE RADIATES LIGHT
LOVE IS LIGHT
UNITY EMERGES
FORGIVENESSS AND COMPASSION
LIVE WITHIN LOVE
JUSTICE LIVES WITHIN LOVE
LOVE IS THE VESSEL FOR JUSTICE
TO KNOW JUSTICE
IS TO BE LOVE
JUSTICE EMERGES
LOVE IS JUSTICE

MYSTERY OF LIFE

I AM AGELESS
   NO TIME AND SPACE
I BREATHE ETERNAL LIFE
   I EMBODY DIVINITY
MY TRUE ESSENCE
   IS THE ELIXIR OF MAGIC

I DANCE THE SPIRAL OF LOVE
   THE DANCE OF THE UNIVERSE
AS I BREATHE, I HARMONIZE
   WITH THE UNIVERSAL RHYTHM
SO MYSTIC THIS SACRED DANCE
   THE SECRET OF LIFE

JUST PAUSE AND BREATHE
   CLOSE YOUR EYES
FEEL THE VIBRATION
   IN YOUR CELLS
WHISPERS OF NATURE
   AWAKEN YOUR INNER WISDOM
SO MAGICAL THE MYSTERY OF LIFE

INVISIBLE

I TRANSCEND
   FEAR OF THE UNKNOWN
I ALLOW THE UNIVERSE
   TO HOLD MY HAND
I CLOSE MY EYES
   AND LISTEN
ECHOS OF TRUTH
   WHISPER IN MY EARS

I LIVE IN THE ETERNAL MOMENT
   A VESSEL FILLED WITH LOVE
ECSTASY IS MY PLEASURE
   ON THIS MAGICAL JOURNEY
I DANCE THE SPIRAL OF LOVE
   WEAVING A NEW TAPESTRY
I AM FLEXIBLE
   I SEE THE INVISIBLE

BUTTERFLY

I AM A BUTTERFLY
  I TRAVEL FAR
WHEN I APPEAR
  I TRANFORM SOCIETY
I LIFT UP HUMANITY
  TO LOFTY PLACES

I AM THE LIGHT
  ILLUMINATING
WE STAND UNITED
  IN MAGNIFICENCE
WE ARE THE COCOON
  OF A NEW REALITY

COCOON OF LIFE

AS I SPIN IN MY COCOON
MY WINGS ARE FORMING
I GAZE OUT AT THE WORLD
I SEE CHAOS SPINNING ORDER
THE UNIVERSE'S MAGICAL DANCE
I CHOOSE MY PATH
HONORING MY UNIQUE PURPOSE

UNIVERSAL ORDER IS PRECISION
LISTEN TO THE EARTH'S DRUMBEAT
CALLING US HOME TO UNITY
EACH LANGUAGE HAS A VIBRATION
EACH ANIMAL A FREQUENCY
AS WE SING IN UNISON
WE HARMONIZE ONENESS

AS I BURST FROM MY COCOON
FLUTTERING MY WINGS
GLIDING THROUGH THE AIR
I MARVEL AT THE MAGESTY OF NATURE
I AM A LIVING LIGHT
MY VIBRATION AWAKENS
IN ALL WHO GAZE UPON MY WINGS

SPIRIT OF PEACE

SEE THE LIGHT
   THIS IS ENLIGHTMENT
FEEL UNCONDITIONAL LOVE
   THIS IS THE SPIRIT OF PEACE
SURRENDER TO THE UNSEEN
   THIS IS FREEDOM

MAGIC OF LIFE

LOOK THROUGH THE EYES OF TRUTH
   FIND YOUR HUMANITY
THIS IS WHERE LIBERATION LIVES
   WE ARE THE MASTERS OF OUR WORLD
THIS FLOW OF ENERGY IS OUR WINGS
   THE GUIDING FORCE
WE HOLD THE KEY WITHIN
   TO HEAL HUMANITY AND THE EARTH

KNOW THYSELF

I SEEK MY UNKNOWN SELF
I PARTICIPATE IN LIFE
I LIVE IN GRATITUDE
I SEARCH FOR TRUTH
I TRUST MY INTUITION

I KNOW MYSELF
I SEE THE UNSEEN
I HAVE ALL I DESIRE
I AM LOVE IN ACTION
I EXPERIENCE YOU

VEIL OF PERCEPTION

OUR PERCEPTIONS FORM REALITY
A VEIL CONCEALS THE FOG
WHEN I SEE TRUTH
MY PERCEPTION SHIFTS
THE VEIL IS LIFTED IN MY MIND
I SEE NEW POSSIBILITIES
LOVE CREATES NEW REALITIES
NOW TRUTH PREVAILS

FREEDOM

FREEDOM IS A STATE OF BEING
   THAT LIVES IN MY HEART
FREEDOM IS KNOWING THE TRUTH
   AND BEING IN ACTION
WHEN MY HEART BURSTS FREE
   NO WALL CAN CONTAIN IT
NO OUTSIDE FORCE
   CAN TAKE IT AWAY

FREEDOM IS A CHOICE
   TO HONOR MY RESPONSIBIITY
AS CONSCIOUS ARCHITECT
   OF MY REALITY
I MUST HAVE FREEDOM WITHIN
   TO EXPERIENCE IT ON THE OUTSIDE
IT MEANS LETTING GO
   AND LIVING IN THE MOMENT

NELSON MANDELA

HIS BIRTH NAME WAS MADIBA
  MEANING FATHER
HIS PURPOSE WAS TO BE
  THE FATHER OF HUMANITY'S FREEDOM
HE MODELED GREAT LEADERSHIP
  TO LEADING FROM BEHIND

HE KNEW TO BE FREE
    WE MUST LIBERATE THE OPPRESSOR
      AND THE OPPRESSED
  YOU FREE YOURSELF FROM WITHIN
    THROUGH FORGIVENESS
HE KNEW IT IS OUR CHOICE TO BE ANGRY OR FREE
  THOUGHTS AND FEELINGS THAT IGNITE ANGER
    DO NOT ALLOW TRUTH AND FREEDOM
    TO LIVE IN OUR HEARTS

HE CONNECTED WITH THE HEARTS
  OF HIS OPPRESSORS
HE COMMUNICATED
  FROM A HIGHER LEVEL OF CONSCIOUSNESS
  UNDERSTOOD THIS IS THE PATH TO FREEDOM
  LIVED IN GRACE, DIGNITY AND COURAGE
HE EMBODIED THE ESSENCE OF FREEDOM
  FOR HUMANITY
HIS PHYSICAL DEATH RELEASES HIS ENERGY
  OF BEING FREEDOM FOR HUMANITY
THANK YOU FOR YOUR PRESENCE ON EARTH
WE HONOR YOU
  FOR BEING THE ESSENCE OF FREEDOM

DIVINE ORDER

ALL IS IN DIVINE ORDER
ALL IS PERFECTION
THE MAGIC OF LIFE IS IN THE INFINITE
WHEN WE CLOSE OUR EYES
DIMENSIONS OF OUR SOULS ARE VISIBLE
CONNECTING US
  TO THE UNIVERSAL MATRIX

AS WE SPIN IN THE VORTEX OF INFINITY
INVISIBLE POSSIBILITIES ARE VISIBLE
WE SPIN DIVINE ORDER OUT OF CHAOS
NEW STRUCTURES FORM
  FROM WITHIN ONENESS
THEN OUTWARD THROUGH LOVE
IN OUR HEARTS WE ARE ONE

SOAR LIKE AN EAGLE

THERE IS MAGIC
  INSIDE OF YOU
    WAITING TO BE BORN
YOUR INNER WISDOM
  IS YOUR GUIDE
    LEADING YOU UPWARD
ASK THE UNIVERSE
  FOR THE CALL

WHEN YOU ARE ASKED
  JUMP OFF THE CLIFF
FLY WITH WINGS
  SOAR LIKE AN EAGLE
THE WIND WILL GLIDE YOU
  HIGH ABOVE THE STORM
YOU WILL BE GRACED
  WITH COURAGE

PAINTING

A PAINTING TELLS A STORY
  OF A 1000 WORDS
EXPRESSING IN IMAGES
  LIFE EXPERIENCES
CAPTURING EMOTIONS

THE ARTIST BREATHES
  LIFE INTO THE CANVAS
WITH BRUSH AND COLOR

THE BEHOLDER
  OBSERVES THE MASTERPIECE
THROUGH THE FILTER
  OF THEIR PERCEPTIONS
THE IMAGES IN THE MIND
  ARE THE REFLECTIONS
    OF THESE PERCEPTIONS

INVISIBLE KNOWING

OUR EARTH EXPERIENCE IS "FREE WILL"
THUS, WE CHOOSE OUR REALITY
ASK THE UNIVERSE FOR ASSISTANCE
BE CLEAR WITH YOUR INTENTIONS
OUR HIGHER SELF...
   MANIFESTS EXPERIENCES
THAT CREATE AN "EYE" IN THE STORM
"ALL KNOWING" IS VISIBLE
SURRENDER TO THE PEACE AND CALM
HEREIN...
   IS THE PORTAL TO YOUR GUIDING LIGHT
ONLY IN DARKNESS IS LIGHT VISIBLE
THIS LIGHT IS YOUR GUIDING FORCE
THANK THE UNIVERSE
   FOR THE DARKNESS
GRATITUDE IS THE BRIDGE

HUMMINGBIRD

I BRING LOVE, HAPPINESS AND JOY
  WHEN I CROSS YOUR PATH
I AM THE 'FLYING JEWEL'
  I TRANSCEND TIME AND SPACE
I HEAL WITH LIGHT
  AS A LASER FROM MY MOUTH
I FLY INTO SMALL PLACES
I HAVE ENDURANCE
  FOR LONG JOURNEYS
MY MESSAGE IS POTENT
I NEVER LOOK BACK
  AT WHAT MIGHT HAVE BEEN
I AM ALL POSSIBILITIES

ALCHEMY OF PEACE

I AM AN ORACLE
   HIGH IN THE TEMPLE
PEOPLE COME FROM FAR
   TO SEEK MY WISDOM

I AM THE MASTER
   MY HEART IS THE TEMPLE
THE ORACLE LIVES WITHIN
   WISDOM RADIATES FORTH

I AM THE VOICE OF THE DIVINE
   SOARING ON THE WINGS OF LOVE
WHISPERING IN EARS OF LEADERS
   THE ALCHEMY OF PEACE

WATER

COMMANDER OF OUR SHIP

WE COMMAND OUR DESTINY
  WE CHART OUR PATH
DESTINY IS OUR LIFE PURPOSE
  IT IS OUR CHOICE TO ACCEPT
THIS REQUIRES COMMITMENT
  INVOKING OUR INTENTION
OUR INTENTION COMMANDS
  THE ELEMENTS OF NATURE
THUS ORCHESTRATING
  UNIVERSAL LAWS
THIS HARMONIC BOND
  IS OUR SAIL IN THE STORM

SEA SHELL

SEA SHELL IS THE ECHO OF THE UNIVERSE
   SOUND VIBRATION OF THE COSMOS
CLOSE YOUR EYES
   INVISIBLE APPEARS
LISTEN TO THE ECHO
   REMINDING US OF OUR SOURCE

SEA SHELL IS THE SYMBOL OF DIVINE ORDER
   SPIRALING CODES OF CREATION
SACRED GEOMETRY DANCING
   FIBONACCI SERIES SWIRLING
CODES ARE THE KEY
   TO SYMBIOSIS OF LIFE

VIBRATIONAL ECHOS RESONATE IN OUR CELLS
   FEEL NATURE PASS THROUGH YOUR BODY
SEE MAGIC IN THE CREATION PROCESS
   SUCH PROFOUND MYSTICAL BEAUTY
WISDOM OF THE UNIVERSE
   SELF-DESIGNING NEW LIFE

SEA OF LOVE

I AM DIVINE LOVE
I SWIM IN A UNIVERSE OF LOVE
I RADIATE LOVE FROM MY CELLS
MY MOLECULES DANCE
   IN A SEA OF LOVE

I SEE OUR BODIES BECOMING
   PURE ENERGY
MERGING IN A SEA OF LOVE
   SPARKS FLY
EMBRACING EACH OTHER

I SEE THE COLORS
   SO BRILLIANT
THERE IS NO SEPARATION
PURE ENERGY FLOWING
UNITED AS ONE

LIFE IS A CHOICE

I CHOOSE AWARENESS
INTUITION IS MY GUIDE
MYSTERIES OF THE UNIVERSE
FLOW THROUGH MY CELLS
I AM THE MYSTERY OF LIFE
I AM A HOLOGRAM OF THE UNIVERSE

MY HEART BEATS AS ONE
   WITH THE UNIVERSAL HEART
I SWIM FREELY IN A RIVER OF LOVE
I AM A SPECK FLOATING IN THE COSMOS
I HAVE NO BEGINNING AND END
I AM LIMITLESS
I AM INFINITY

I WALK IN THE WORLD
I AM NOT OF THIS WORLD
I CHOOSE THIS HUMAN EXPERIENCE
I TRANSCEND THIS ILLUSION
I CHOOSE CONSCIOUSNESS
I LIVE LIFE AS MY AUTHENTIC SELF

LIVE LIFE

WE HAVE A DREAM
   FOLLOW THE PATH OF LOVE
WE DARE TO IMAGINE A WORLD
   BASED ON INNER PEACE
THE LAW OF LOVE
   UNFOLDS ITS MAGIC
HEREIN IS THE SECRET
   TO TRUE HAPPINESS

I BELIEVE IN YOUR DREAMS
   OUR DREAMS ARE UNITED
ON THE PATH OF LOVE
   WALKING IN COURAGE
DESIRE HAS ITS OWN HEARTBEAT
   AND INTENTION TO LIVE
I DARE TO FEEL LOVE
   AND LIVE LIFE IN JOY

SACRED ESSENCE

FEEL YOUR ESSENCE EXPAND
   YOU ARE MORE THAN YOUR BODY
YOUR BODY IS THE PHYSICAL FORM
   MATCHING YOUR VIBRATION
AS YOUR HEART BEATS WITH THE COSMOS
   YOU ARE ONE WITH THE EARTH

AS YOU LISTEN TO YOUR BODY'S WISDOM
   YOU SNCHRONIZE YOUR BODY RHYTHMS
     WITH THE RHYTHMS OF THE UNIVERSE
ALLOW THE UNIVERSE TO FLOW THROUGH YOU
   FEEL YOUR SACRED ESSENCE
     THIS IS WHERE FREEDOM LIVES

SECRETS OF LIFE

WHEN WE HEAL OUR HEARTS
   BREATHE WITH THE EARTH
   LISTEN TO SILENCE
   LIVE IN GRATITUDE
   LIVE IN THE MOMENT
THESE ARE THE SECRETS OF LIFE

PEACE, FREEDOM AND JUSTICE
   LIVE IN OUR HEARTS
FROM WITHIN COMES OUR MAGNIFICENCE
   DARE TO DREAM FROM HERE
MAGIC WILL UNFOLD

PHILANTHROPY

THE SECRET OF ABUNDANCE
   IS GRATITUDE AND GIVING
WHEN WE GIVE FREELY
   WITHOUT ATTACHMENT
WE SHIFT THE VIBRATION
   OPENING THE FLOOD GATES
     FOR RECEIVING

PHILANTHROPY IS AN EXCHANGE OF LOVE
   THE GREATEST JOY IS IN GIVING
THE UNIVERSE SUPPORTS US
   WHEN WE COMMIT TO SHARING OUR GIFTS
     AND FOLLOW OUR HEART'S PASSION
SUCCESS IS OUR CONTRIBUTION
   TO HUMANITY

CONSCIOUSNESS OF UNITY

HAVE THE COURAGE TO ACT
   WE ARE THE CONSCIOUSNESS OF UNITY
IT LIES DEEP IN OUR SOULS
   ABOUT TO BE BIRTHED ON EARTH
CONNECTING US TO OUR SOURCE
   OUR ESSENCE HAS RESILIENCE
WE EACH HAVE UNIQUE EXPRESSIONS
   AND THE POTENTIAL TO TRANSFORM
WHEN WE STAY IN THE PRESENT MOMENT
   THIS IS OUR STATE OF GRACE

TRUTH

GREAT WISDOM SPEAKS THROUGH US
   THE VOICES OF THE DIVINE
WE WALK THE EARTH
   EMBRACING DIVERSITY
TRUTH DOES NOT TAKE SIDES
   IT SETS US FREE

TRUTH IS THE KEY TO TRANSFORMATION
   FOR CRISES ARE THE DOORS
THROUGH WHICH THE OLD DISSOLVES
   AND A NEW FOUNDATION ARISES
FOR COMMUNITY AND HARMONY
   TO EVOLVE

SACRED POLITICS

WE EACH ARE PARTICIPANTS
   AS INDIVIDUALS, IN SOCIETY
BY THE WAY WE LIVE OUR LIVES
   AND THE ACTIONS WE TAKE
WEAVING THE FABRIC
   OF CULTURE AND SOCIETY
WE ARE RESPONSIBLE FOR THE POLITICS
   OF GOVERNMENT AND POLICY

SACRED POLITICS IS OUR DUTY
   TO CONSCIOUSLY COCREATE
NEW COMPASSIONATE POLITICS
   CALLING FORTH JUSTICE
FORMING NEW SOCIAL STRUCTURES
   BASED ON UNITY AND DIVERSITY
SACRED POLITICS IS THE UNDERSTANDING
   THAT POLITICS REFLECT OUR INNER BEING

LIBERATION

WHEN YOU RELEASE ILLUSIONS
SPACE IS CLEARED FOR CLARITY
LIBERATION COMES FROM WITHIN
AUTHENTIC POWER IS LOVE POWER
LOVE YOURSELF, LIVE IN TRUTH
BE HEARTFELT ACTION

COMMITMENT TO LOVE IS RESPONSIBILITY
OWNERSHIP OF DIVINE PLAN IS WITHIN
HEAR THE VOICE OF YOUR WISDOM
FEEL THE EMBRACE OF SELF-LOVE
HONOR YOURSELF THE MASTERPIECE
POWER OF LOVE IS LIBERATION

JUSTICE

JUSTICE HONORS ALL HUMANITY
   WITH COMPASSION AND DIGNITY
SOCIAL JUSTICE IS HUMAN RIGHTS
   AND EQUALITY
THE FORCES LEADING US FORWARD
   TO A CONSCIOUS SOCIETY

JUSTICE IS NATURAL LAW
   GOVERNING THE UNIVERSE
AS UNIVERSAL FAMILY MEMBERS
   WE ARE RESPONSIBLE
TO HONOR OUR SACRED DUTY
   TO LIVE IN JUSTICE AND PEACE

VEIL IS LIFTED

THE VEIL IS LIFTED FOR ETERNITY
WE SEE THE TRUTH
WE ARE FROM ONE SOURCE
ONE HUMAN FAMILY
PART OF UNIVERSAL INTELLIGENCE
DANCING THE SPIRAL OF LIFE
WE CREATE A NEW REALITY
OUR HEARTS MERGING
RESONATING AS ONE IN HARMONY

LEADERSHIP

TO SERVE OUR HIGHER PURPOSE IS TO LEAD
THIS IS AUTHENTIC LEADERSHIP
THIS IS THE POWER OF LOVE
CALLING FORTH OUR HEART'S PASSION

OUR HEART IS THE MASTER
BEATING IN HARMONY
WITH THE UNIVERSAL HEART
ONE SOURCE, ONE LOVE

MYSTICISM

THE JOURNEY OF LIFE
   REMEMBERING YOUR HIGHER SELF
AWARENESS OF YOUR AUTHENTIC SELF
   SEEKING YOUR UNIQUE GIFT
ASK, "WHO AM I?"
   AND "WHY AM I HERE?"
THE ANSWERS ARE WITHIN
   YOUR MYSTICAL EXPRESSING ESSENCE

MUSE

MY GUIDING SPIRIT
   SOURCE OF INSPIRATION
THANK YOU FOR ASSISTING
   WITH CRYSTAL LIGHT
YOU ARE MY INNER STRENGTH
   INTERWEAVING THE HIDDEN WORLD
I MASTER DESTINY
   MAGNETIZING MY TRUE SELF

JUST BE

BECOME WHAT YOU DESIRE IN LIFE
YOUR ENERGY RADIATES HEART'S DESIRE
THE LAW OF ATTRACTION
 REFLECTS BACK TO YOU YOUR DESIRE
WE HAVE EVERYTHING WITHIN OURSELVES
SO JUST BE!

TRUE POWER

TRUE POWER IS INNER POWER
   ACCESSING OUR INTUITIVE WISDOM
THE ABILITY TO MANIFEST ANYTHING
   TO CREATE THE INVISIBLE
STANDING IN COURAGE AND BOLDNESS
   TO DREAM THE IMPOSSIBLE
WALKING FORWARD WITH NO STRUCTURE
   KNOWING WE ARE THE SOURCE
BREATHING IN UNISON WITH THE UNIVERSE
   BIRTHING A NEW HUMANITY

MIRRORS OF MY HEART

I TRANSCEND LIMITED BELIEF
   AND FEAR OF SEPARATION
I ALLOW THE SYNERGY
   OF LIFE TO UNFOLD
MY DREAMS REVEAL MIRACLES
   I MANIFEST THEM INTO FORM

I GIVE OF MYSELF
   COURAGEOUSLY ACTING
MY HEART IS OPEN
   TO RECEIVE ABUNDANCE
THE MIRRORS OF MY HEART
   REFLECT LOVE AND JOY

GRATITUDE

BE IN GRATITUDE
   THE ELIXIR OF MAGIC
THE VIBRATION
   OF ALL POSSIBILITIES
TRANSFORMING LIFE
   INTO NEW REALITIES

SACRED MISSION

A DANCE OF EGO AND SPIRIT
  WHAT WILL YOU CHOOSE
FOLLOW YOUR INNER WISDOM
  IT ALWAYS SPEAKS TRUTH
YOU HAVE A SACRED MISSION

IF YOU SHOW UP
  YOUR LIFE WILL BE BEAUTIFUL
IF YOU LOOK FOR LOVE COURAGOUSLY
  IT WILL REVEAL ITSELF
LIFE WILL BE EXTRAORDINARY

PURPOSE OF LIFE

LIFE IS TO BE LOVE
  THEN I CAN LOVE
WHEN I LOVE MYSELF
  I LOVE LIFE

My hope is that the sacred poems in this book expand your consciousness and lead you to higher knowledge. Know whatever you are experiencing in this moment you are co-creating with universal intelligence to clear old belief patterns and activate your life purpose. We choose the threads of life that weave our matrix of experiences. You are supported by the universal heart/mind. You are crafting your unique signature of the universal matrix. You are love.

Emerald

www.ingramcontent.com/pod-product-compliance
Lightning Source LLC
Chambersburg PA
CBHW042053290426
44110CB00006B/165